To: Al + Fran
from: John D.

A collection of my sister's
work for

Watershed

the "Little Library"

July 4, 2015

Watershed

poems

Laura Donnelly

Cider Press Review
San Diego

WATERSHED

Copyright © 2014 by Laura Donnelly. All rights reserved. No part of this book may be reproduced or utilized in any manner whatsoever without written permission, except in the case of brief quotations embodied in critical articles and reviews. Inquiries should be addressed to:

> *Cider Press Review*
> PO BOX 33384
> San Diego, CA, USA
> CIDERPRESSREVIEW.COM

First edition
10 9 8 7 6 5 4 3 2 1 0

ISBN: 978-1-930781-16-0
Library of Congress Control Number: 2014943338

Cover art, *Pytelia nitidula = Mandingoa nitidula* (1910) by Henrik Gronvold, courtesy wikicommons.org
Author photograph by Keech Photography
Cover design by Caron Andregg

ABOUT THE *CIDER PRESS REVIEW* EDITORS' PRIZE:

The annual *Cider Press Review* Editors' Prize offers a $1,000 prize, publication, and 25 author's copies of a book-length collection of poetry. For complete guidelines and information, visit CIDERPRESSREVIEW.COM/BOOKAWARD.

Printed in the United States of America
at Thomson-Shore, in Dexter, MI.

For my mother

And for Ben

Contents

Acknowledgments　　　　　　　　　　　　　　vii

I
Anamnesis　　　　　　　　　　　　　　　　　3
Darwin's Finches　　　　　　　　　　　　　　4
Foal　　　　　　　　　　　　　　　　　　　　7
The Dove House　　　　　　　　　　　　　　8
Once, in the door of　　　　　　　　　　　　11
Knife-grinder: Principle of Flickering (1913)　　13
Letter from Stonington　　　　　　　　　　　18
Toccata or Fugue　　　　　　　　　　　　　　20
You walk into a room　　　　　　　　　　　　21

II
Driving Home to Sirens　　　　　　　　　　　25
Saint Reparata　　　　　　　　　　　　　　　26
My mother walks from the water　　　　　　27
Possum　　　　　　　　　　　　　　　　　　28
The Same Story　　　　　　　　　　　　　　29
Intermezzo　　　　　　　　　　　　　　　　30
To Fanny Mendelssohn　　　　　　　　　　　31
Three Poems　　　　　　　　　　　　　　　　34
After the Divorce　　　　　　　　　　　　　　37
Reading Thomas Hardy　　　　　　　　　　　39
Wintering (January)　　　　　　　　　　　　40
The Goldberg Variations　　　　　　　　　　41
Unlatching　　　　　　　　　　　　　　　　　42

III

Sacrament	45
Ways of Entering Water	46
Instructions for the Binoculars	48
Notes on the Appositive	51
Watershed	53
Exploring the Island	57
Tuning A	58
Suspension	59
The Bathers	62
Late Winter	63
The Coefficient of Longing	64
The Piano	65
Notes	69

Acknowledgments

Grateful acknowledgment is made to the following journals, in which poems from this manuscript appeared:

Black Tongue Review: "Coefficient of Longing," "Ways of Entering Water"
Cider Press Review: "Notes on the Appositive"
Cimarron Review: "Darwin's Finches," "Knife-grinder: Principle of Flickering (1913)," "Once, in the door of"
CutBank: "To Fanny Mendelssohn"
Flyway: "Foal," "Wintering (January)"
DMQ Review: "Anamnesis," "Possum"
Georgetown Review: "Letter from Stonington"
Poetry East: "Late Winter," "The Piano," "Unlatching"
Portland Review: "Toccata or Fugue"
Rhino: "The Dove House"
Third Coast: "Driving Home to Sirens"
Sakura Review: "The Bathers"
Weave: "Saint Reparata"

"Intermezzo" and "Tuning A" first appeared in the chapbook *Nocturne—Schumann's Letters* (Finishing Line Press, 2010).

Thank you to Nancy Eimers, Jennifer K. Sweeney, and Katherine Bode-Lang for helping me find this book's shape. And to Priscilla Atkins and Beth Marzoni for close readings of many of these poems. Thanks also to a host of wonderful teachers: Marianne Boruch, William Olsen, Donald Platt, Jack Ridl, Joan Conway, Jackie Bartley, and many others for their invaluable guidance. Thank you to Rebekah Silverman, Beth Lyons, Christine Haskell, Beth and Roger Kolp, and Elizabeth Kolp for their friendship and support. Most of all, my love and gratitude to my parents and brother. And to Ben, always.

I am deeply grateful to Caron Andregg and Ruth Foley at *Cider Press Review* for believing in this collection. And to the inspiring faculty and students at the State University of New York at Oswego, Knox College, Western Michigan University, and Purdue University.

This work was supported by residencies at Ragdale and Yaddo, and by a Dissertation Fellowship at Western Michigan University.

I

Anamnesis

Not forgetting the swing set's
old ropes, the park blinking fireflies.

Not forgetting the dance, applause
through the band shell. And later,

fireworks from the pier, small bombs
in our chests. Not forgetting

how we lay on rough woolen blankets,
up late for the show, junior high girls

with ankles and wrists overlapping.
Not forgetting even our not-knowing,

its breakable cup in our hands.
So much I make up—*the paper-dry wind*—

or, past that—*our pink throats opened up.*
Not real, but how like the invisible spires

of sailboats, each floating a single
green light below so much smoke,

their constellations drawn to us.

Darwin's Finches

The Galapagos Islands. Gnarled
    beaks of the finches'

quick change. *Woodpecker finch,*
    warbler finch, the brightly

sharp-beaked. My mother
    never went there, researched

the blunt-billed *cactus finch*
    a continent away.

Lost years ago from the mainland,
    they stayed on these islands

that made them become something
    else. Generations

of climate change, food change.
    My mother, her

biologist self, says, *Just look*
    at those beautiful beaks.

———

Of course it is something so small.

Lizard feet. Clawed toes.
Those black eyes. It's the beaks though

that show it. As hunger has always had a way
of taking precedence.

———

A young woman reading ledger
after ledger of field work. Not me
but my mother.
                      Her library's alcoves
I imagine, though I've seen the books too.

In one photo—hard seeds, the dry season.
In another—just the thickening
of beaks.

The birds unconcerned, or rather
so concerned they no longer have to think it.

———

I dream birds everywhere. In her long hair,
of course, in her eye.

The faulty roof drips in the entryway,
living room, bedroom, and they are

everywhere looking for a foothold.
They lift off the pier, stalk

through the parking lot looking for trash.
They are everywhere

singing and not singing.

———

Yellow gold, speckled
black, garnet red in winter.
Birds come to my mother's feeder.

She grows older. Like her grandmother,
never lets the feeder go empty.

It can take forever to lure them back.

When my students complain
about long assignments, I tell them
my mother wrote fifty pages about finches,
just their beaks. I want to tell them
something about desire.

Foal

The thing that wants to be born
is turned sideways and stiffening.

You must twist the head, thread
the flexible cartilage and pull

until the forehoof relaxes.
The mare's heaves will crush

your shoulder, crush the night
into rough shards of stable and moon,

but once all is loosed you won't feel
the kneading pain. Pain, they say,

makes you stronger, but that isn't it—
You and the mother splayed out

on your sides, watching the foal
breathe into newly damp hay.

The Dove House

after Winslow Homer's Cullercoats paintings

All down the wharf the women
mend nets and this song on the radio,
I remember it too. The hooks on the lines
like so many small fingers. The oysters' sheen
clapped shut and burred into place.

———

Aged fifteen, they claimed, a shilling a day
for her straight back, straight chin. Maggie on break
from mending the nets. Not more
than *thirteen*, but already those steel-pinned eyes
gone to market, steel voice hawking herring.
Bright sun against slate, barrel shimmered
with scales. She wears the woven basket
like a third hip tilted wide.

———

The men leave every night. The moon,
should there be one, calling the fish
like a lover.
         Meanwhile the painter
might sleep. Every blue on the palette a shadow,
black hole, and the quiet is such a fine echo.

———

A border, a shoreline, a wandering sheer.

Whoever has dropped
in storm, in darkness, and how the salt tastes
bone-deep loss.
                       To cross over and back
as if into dream. To wade deeply. To grasp

barefoot the breakwater and fossil
yourself to that wall.

———

Sway out the sails, the billowing gray-
blue skirt, overskirt,
how I always think of sky as *fabric*.

Our shoulders seep up watercolor
the way waves take the changeling sky.
This line a whole note, a full breath.

When the mainsail expands,
the chest with it. *Weight, counterweight. Weight,
counterweight.* The wind creates
peaks and troughs in the sky. Sea spray
about to tear paper.

———

Every hole in your life. The ones you made,
the ones handed down. The sea that will swallow
your father, your brother. There are stitches for this,
the needle's quick dive down-and-back
not a sliver of gray but a thick slab of bone.

You imagine your life a long, low boat
and the tide a barely perceptible iron glow.

For *dove,* for sparrow: gray softness
of flight.

For the cliff edge: these years
looking up, out, and over,
that ruddy-cheeked squint in the sun.

And for *house:* stoic keeper, stone on stone,
Sparra Harl, you grasp at the name's guttural,

how we perch there between rock and flight.

Once, in the door of

summer on a midland bank,
for no good reason in England, a village,
the end of the twentieth century
suddenly looking so like the beginning—
a manor house, the guidebook said,
a quarter mile down the path.
For no good reason, and yet
it has to be here because here is
in memory and I want this
accurate, an opening
in the stone wall—see?—light dazzling
my camera from the other side
so it cannot make out the gravel,
hedgerow, exposure with crystalline spots
like the time when I stared too long at the sun
though they warned us not to,
huge *they* of adulthood who guided us
through our first solar eclipse,
pinpricks in thick paper viewfinders,
enough just to let that much through, to see—
what were we supposed to see? Today,
or not today but much closer to it, sunlight
hit leaves turned up like the surprised
underbelly of seaweed, a secret raised, and me only
sixteen—*no,* because this wants accuracy,
eighteen, but still so young and in love with
everything. Someone says, *You were
too much alone.* Someone says, *Old world
anachronisms,* but in my mind
I'm still standing before this *once,
rosebush, wonder*—words to tuck

like slate stones in my pockets. *It will shatter
if you walk through,* someone warns.
It would shatter if I didn't.

Knife-grinder: Principle of Flickering (1913)

> *The title itself,* Principle of Flickering, *refers to Malevich's abandonment of the physical object.... About this time the physical theory of waves was developed, which no longer interpreted the world as static.*
>
> —Jeannot Simmen, *Malevich, Life and Work*

It's as simple as saying we move, we are
        constantly moving, and
                someone wanted to show that
the oddest way, a painting's taut canvas

still as the building in which this man sits
        at his knife-grinder's wheel,
                fingers like blunt sticks
of chalk, not hands now but tools, all tuned

to a world's glancing edge.
        In the book at home you show how
                Malevich has painted
the man's wooden mustache on once, twice,

at least four times while his bent elbow jigsaws
        consecutive frames
                simultaneously,
foot thrumming as if at an organ's bellows

this music that makes a stone spin.
        Difficult not to freeze the man
                to a certainty
where we nod at labors gone by.

What you don't say (what, perhaps,
        you don't know):
                Malevich himself
is doing away with the object, on his way

towards a looming black square
        with which he will frighten
                a country that stands
at the edge of war, *Great—, World—,*

he will pace his room, nights, with that square
        in his head, an answer
                to a world flickering
on and off without reason, a country

thrumming its frozen-most corners—
        a black square is where this is going.

―

Today I am watching Pablo Casals,
        or rather, looking at this photo—
                Casals with his cello,
eyes lowered to half-moons—and listening

to a CD of him patched together
        from dozens of transfers,
                the cello suites
performed in the 1930's. We're lucky

for such a near seamless collage of him
        moving across Bach's notes,
                which wait always
for someone to touch them again, for that

same, not-quite-same-again flight—
        Like reviving colors
                from a sepia colored photograph,
Suzuki writes in the liner notes, and yet

I have to be critical. . . even Casals was not free
        from the time he lived—

———

At the museum, you call me
        from where I've been standing
                before Bonnard's bathing wife,
titled simply *The Bathroom,* a nude ever leaning

to dry her dark hair, his Marthe suspended
        in pastel. We play this game
                throughout the museum,
sharing our favorites—

they do not have the *Knife-grinder*
        but here is Malevich's
                Woman with Pails,
whose movement has lost all sign of the figure

until, one hand lifted and inches from canvas
        you translate the bell-wide skirt,
                arms swaying beneath the broad yoke
like two white birds attempting flight.

We've both settled ourselves before women
        with water, but what is it
                makes me admire but not love
Malevich's sharp-angled geometry?

Bonnard, says the placard, rarely showed
        his wife's face, but how tenderly
                we follow the part
in her hair, inverted arrow of her body,

moisture fading from still warm feet
        whose lines are blurred, yes,
                but singular—
though I may have imagined the evaporation,

the tiles, the window high over a freestanding tub.
        And did I imagine that detail?
                How he rarely painted her face
because he would leave her that small secrecy?

—

The young Casals in motion decades
        after his death, my first thought
                is how quietly he plays it,
how oddly Romantic. He leaves the studio

in a felt hat tugged low, bottle-thick glasses
        through which the street disappears
            long before the horizon—
he is humming, must be humming, I think,

sotto voce, *Eppur si muove (nonetheless*
        the earth moves). . . a tune almost like
           but not quite this one
I've been listening to all afternoon.

To move through this world *in waves,* my love—
        it's a wonder we cross paths at all.

Letter from Stonington

The clouds stretch milky lines
      across the wharf, blurred

in two places as if rubbed out
      by the artist's fist.

Late afternoon, the harbor fills
      with the gravelly idle

of lobster boats. A hunched man
      in burgundy sweater

maneuvers his low-slung boat
      in reverse, rests one arm

on the gunnel as he stoops
      to gather rope. *The Hermitage*,

I thought his boat read,
      and liked the thought

of the hermit captain until
      Ben corrected me, *Heritage*—

same name given our room
      at the inn. The tourists

have mostly thinned out but those
      remaining take turns

on a narrow pier. High tide today
      came at dawn and dusk.

At noon all the boats were out to sea
        except one that leant

into a dock, its rudder exposed,
        ropes holding it from

the nothingness that the sea
        had filled hours before.

We fought on our way to the island.
        I don't recall why, or I do

now, something about motorcycles
        and death, but it doesn't

bear repeating. I call Ben over
        as the captain takes lobsters

from a tank, lopsided claws
        bound, tails thrashing

as he loads them into the blue and white
        crates that lift overhead.

We pass the binoculars back and forth
        between us. At dusk

the clouds grow less meticulous.
        The flaws, if there are flaws,

more difficult to discern.

Toccata or Fugue

Two strings of the upright piano
snapped,
their corded wire sprung and dangling.

      I learned to expect the dull *thunk*
that went with low E. The music, a moment, weightless

until the chord changed.

Sometimes when I sleep, I still hear that piano.
I dream Brahms in waves or Bach
thrumming rain on my window—
      toccata or fugue, which mean

touch and *flight*—

Touch—I try the rain with cupped hands
but it flies through my fingers.

If my teacher were here now, what would she say?

The hole in the piano—
The wild birds—
The rain?

You walk into a room

1.
You walk into a room. It is dark, or it's barely light on one end—French windows, white casings. Dust motes, as if treading water, tread light. To your right, shadows. To your left, sheets covering monstrous shapes. Exposed, they'd be ordinary enough. A table with a lamp, a chair and its stool.

2.
You walk into a room. This time the light is rosy—sunlight through the webbing of fingers or rust-red dahlias bent low by their beauty. You walk into a room and you say, *Love, tie my hair back.* You walk into a room and you say, *Beyond these walls the birds are calling their names.*

3.
At the end of the room, a window. Through the window sunlight hits filaments of cobweb and no sign of where this silk anchors. Strange trick of light, trick of space. Spiders lacing themselves to the sky.

4.
Once, in Paris, you leaned into that light's long sigh. You made a shadow in a photo, tall and too thin. You remember this girl. You leaned into that light for less than one day, then were gone. You have no photo of being gone.

5.
So you walk through the prairie, try the woods. You take the bike with the rattling chain to town and pray you won't spill. You spill. And *spill, from* spel: *to split or break off*—but you bring the room with you, a shoulder bag flopping against one side as you pump the pedals like a fool, like no child you recall though you know the wind on your wet face.

6.

You walk into a room as if entering under a gray-white canopy and then the canopy removed, the sky closer than expected. Now if you want flight, you must pump your arms madly. If you want flight, you must choose it. Close your eyes and light's climbing the finest cobwebs to nothing.

II

Driving Home to Sirens

I learn anger like a stone thrown
into a tree when all I had wanted

was to bind the tree up with twine—
the broken bird beak, torn nest,

tangled twigs. At heart, I'm still sick
of things cracking but these stones

sink, heavy to fly. This cut glass is no
sugar spoon, no kaleidoscope,

these ambulances real, every night
and the police cars close behind.

My father explains, *It's hard to prosecute
when the women always retract.* This time,

three counts, hands bound to the chair,
gun brushing the pillowcased head. Later,

a drunken man ass-over-teakettle
in the yard calling for forgiveness. Call it

a Band-Aid, but oh—this nest is a hive, and
I'd crash my car to join that siren's wail.

Saint Reparata

Open mouth and the dove emerging from lips,
her head thrown back in the strange birth—

then her body packed into a shallow skiff and wind
pushing towards sanctity. Child martyr,

her vaults have been buried by that greater virgin,
Holy Mother ascendant, Maria del Fiore,

still the hills of Fiesole recall her lily-white,
palms waving for the girl forgotten, girl-Daniel,

entering the fire and not a burn, her flesh cool
among the embers. So why did it work

when they chopped off her head? The wonder
of the miracle gone fickle. I imagine a city, doves

in every mouth and flight overtaking the sky.
And what of the body that floats? Brushing the edges

of the Arno or endlessly circling a sun-blanched sea?
Easy to accept the dissolve of Assumption, Mary

gazing heavenward, glistening light,
but this boat-swollen body concerns me.

World no longer flat, I've seen how the wind blowing
one direction comes back to haunt from another.

My mother walks from the water

in a lurid purple bikini, orange
hibiscus petals blossoming over her.
Nearby, debris in the surf: a plastic bag,

a muddied shirt. All of it in the heat
she hates. Here, fifteen years
before she'll leave, she walks towards

a camera my father must hold.
They never appear together. Always one
or the other as if prescience bade them

take turns. She tells me it wasn't paradise,
tourists clogging the beach, jellyfish
like limp sacks on the sand. How she knew

even then it wouldn't work out.
Now the family photos stack in drawers
where my niceness strives against

this not-paradise, not accepted,
not acceptable lens. *Is it too much to ask?*
Usually. But I'd wish them an evening

breeze, all the same. A sunset to ignore
how everything that should have been lush
was already straggling up to shore.

Possum

First, the hanging feeder fell
        when the squirrel swung from its grate.

We watched the cardinals light on the mess,
        peck seeds from the snow.

Then the sound of a woodpecker
        far in the field. We could say of these,

Signs of spring, but here snow
        stays late into April. Nothing blossoms,

nothing will shake its lilac jackets to the ground
        like snow. There is only real snow.

We place bets: when the ice will melt off the lake, when
        the possum will come to the sliding glass door

in the night, pressing its nose, showing its teeth
        in a monstrous yawn. But we take it

for what it is—not omen.

The Same Story

Children wearing moon boots
tromp by my house
and I think of the way I once followed
my brother, tugging a silver saucer
back from the hill. Both of us
falling deep in snow, leaving our lunar prints.

It was always dusk. It was always
a long way to go. Past Aunt Jan's pond,
past her row of bird houses
on steeple-tall poles. I sunk
my hands in a pan of tepid water
until they stung. Then hot cocoa
and Mother saying, *Not so long next time.*
Scarves and snow pants draped
over the registers, dirty snow
turning to steam.

Intermezzo

> *Can you tell me why we are sometimes*
> *so blissfully happy in this world?*
>
> —Robert Schumann

Once, the tower clock
ringing midnight, the rain-
blackened cobbles,
the perfect round weight
of a doorknocker in his hand.
Once he was a young man walking
back to the boarding house, yes
with a song in his head,
everything with a song, a lieder
for Clara who practiced
piano in the room beside his own,
all of it like the first half
of the film that sets you up
to feel worse in the end. The hand
mangled, the brain
addled, which means today
so desperate you'd do
anything. Then: bloodletting,
or "breathing a vein,"
the forearm's red ache in the basin.

To Fanny Mendelssohn

In the low egg yolk morning she is trying
        to dissolve the bar lines,
                mathematical placements
with which she is told she lives

            too much in her mind. She wants
this to feel like song, possibility
              become effortless:
      the robin's chitter, a field.

But each morning the family's pianoforte
        slides further out of tune.
           Each morning
in the picture window, the rhythm of

           practice room, stranglehold.
(But no—was that *me?* What she feels,
            how to say?) I imagine
    an opaque window, sunlight

through waxy paper.

———

Her brother visits from Vienna. She paints watercolors.
      Pale spring hills, the lake valley,
           beside her the water jar
clouds over blue, aqua, gold. The brush shaken clean

                between colors. It is not a bad life.
Her brother's *Songs Without Words,*
                        of which many are hers,
     are publishable with his name.

Queen Victoria's favorite, "Italy," is Fanny's own.
            She gives concerts at home,
                    notes echoing over marble
like quick, clipped footsteps.

———

So many writers on hands: *Her small neat hands.*
      Her white hands.
                Her marble hands. He fell out of love
because her hands appeared larger.

                I'm beginning to think the mechanics
mean little. I sit in the heat of August
                    watching how hands work.
      Science of the smallest joints

that do or do not do my bidding by rote. In the end
     it only works when you learn to forget.

———

What if not remembered, not graphed
        on the music staff's bars like those leaps
                once charting my heartbeat? (Even
as a child I knew something was wrong, lying on the bed

        while the EKG jolted off-
rhythm, off-kilter, what kept me on edge—)
                What if in sleep, in first waking,
      those colors of the water jar blurred,

the lake's depths and murmurs, its blue eye merging
        towards gray still swirling
                around the brush bristles I shake?
What if so worried (then)

                to get it right—
scale after skeleton scale and so far from the flesh
                of the piece, I only begin
        to know what it was I heard—

Three Poems

1. In the Uffizi

Drape of smooth stone,
      white stare of eyeballs
never painted—or painted
      and long since rubbed back
to blankness. Marble torsos
      cool to the touch.
Mostly they don't face each other
      or us, retaining poses
from *before:* Diana intent
      on the stag we don't see,
Apollo mourning Hyacinth,
      down on both knees,
we imagine the archer before him.
      Then so many unnamed—
this one bent over her missing jug,
      sharp chin, shoulders
tensed, again she lowers to lift.

2. Botticelli's *Annunciation,* Hospital of San Martino alla Scala

All we saw was a wash of pastel—
        pink blur of Gabriel's robes
then the scaffolding softened
        by painter's cloths. Quiet arc
of the Virgin's brow. We followed
        the cordoned paths
through barely lit vaults, empty brick
        surgeries—a shelf where
a basin for bloodletting rested, a forceps.
        And what of the doctors?
What did they think, being told
        each day of the miracle?
Between her and Gabriel a column
        of paint rubbed away, cracked
walls where typhoid once lingered
        below the good angel.

3. Botticelli's *Allegory of Spring*

They dance, the Graces,
        feet overlapping, soft line
of callus on heel, gowns sheer
        as wind grazing ankles.
So many longhaired women
        caught in Spring's movement—
Zephyr, the west wind, hovers
        scowling and blue, though
only the nearest one turns back
        in fear. Naked and stumbling,
garland flows from her mouth like
        fish line. Her twin stands nearby
in thick brocade, smiles forgetfully,
        his hands already on her, his
blue touch that's already changing
        her to someone else.

After the Divorce

In a town of platitudes
and tulips and a wooden shoe festival,
we started our family
again, more concerned with a summer
pool pass and lack of new tennis shoes
than our father's sudden absence.

I think it was worse for you,
being older and male—
by which I mean, *see
how generous I've grown?*
We battled each other,
and later you blackened the eyes
of your junior high classmates.

When I last visited, we drove
to the lake where we're both
most at home, your new Jeep
big enough for five kids
and a dog, though I know
how you don't want either.
What are we proving, big brother?
(Each time, I stay away longer.)

We hike dunes of shattered sand
to a beach the tourists don't know
and the yacht club ignores,
though I used to prefer to sneak into
their parties, shy in a bright
new swimsuit I couldn't afford.

I'm ashamed of it, now.
I pretended my family away

then bawled like a baby when I moved
to another state. You stayed
and pounded your fists against asphalt
until it answered your will.

Reading Thomas Hardy

The coming together of two people
       is nothing the world makes easy.
It's all sorrow paid by the word
       in this story. Outside,
red leaves in rain paste themselves
       to my window, a symphony
finishes, my house so quiet
       I've forgotten how to sleep.
Why not finish *Jude,* who reminds me
       the first time I said *I love you*
to my love was when I was angry.
       Still, I keep going back—
Sue laughing before Jude's hearth,
       run away through river and rain
and dressed in his second-best suit
       by the fire. Sure they argue,
but we're still whole chapters away
       from the end, that last scene
in the school which I keep wanting to go
       differently, keep wanting to believe
could go—it doesn't matter knowing
       better. Who wouldn't
do it again? The little left in our hands
       given up to the stone gods
knocking our hearts.

Wintering (January)

Geese gone from the park,
the black pond frozen
quiet, though not the pivot
of the stream trailing from.
But the milkweed pods, yes,
their threads frozen to pewter,
the thousand trees trundled
to root. The paths we walked
last November are lost below
three feet of snow, and the dog-
violet, phlox, New England
aster hide away their blue-eyed
rebirth. The animals
we never, or rarely, saw, now
never seen in a new way—
the skunk with her litter
of kits, *not true hibernators,*
but they do *den up, dormant
for extended periods.* And we too
turn inwards, watching
the neighbor's car hidden
by drift until only the sheen
of one wheel suggests motion.
Even the sky grows distant.
All month, the days spread
gauze over the sun and come night
not a sliver to speak of. Soon,
a shiver is all it takes to contract
the entire body, muscle
shuddered to bone,
bone tightening towards
whatever weak flame we tend.

The Goldberg Variations

I'm twenty, listening to Glenn Gould again,
the college library muffled by industrial earphones.

Somewhere along the spinning record,
the grooved lines between variations, the theme

is only a starting point. Crisp baroque notes
separated by hair's breadth silences that expand

and contract into thirty-one variations.
Number irrelevant. What matters is trill, what matters

is counterpoint, four voices deep and each one
its own distinct trail. Sunday mornings,

years later, I'll listen for the theme at the record's edge,
then the aria where it returns, needle gliding

towards some center point. My legs so sore
from waiting tables, I won't want to walk downstairs

to the kitchen but will sit in my room with those silences
still expanding, until going further and further has

nothing to do with anything.

Unlatching

      A small white bird
leaving my hand, or
      the sky unhinged
from the earth
      and the whole horizon
flooding with birds.
      *This is not a song
but a piece,* the teacher says,
      and I see it measured
across the black bars or torn
      like damp newspaper
caught in a storm,
      a piece and a piece
and a piece that I
      would have called *song*
had I not known better.

III

Sacrament

I believe in
        a lake holding us—
how suspension works,
        each nerve ending
lit and yes—light lifting
        the heavy bones.
Do in remembrance
        the body is told
and it does. I stretch my arms
        at my sides,
underwater, to touch you—
        world with end
after end and sometimes,
        string of seaweed,
of pearl—We call this
        meanwhile—Call this
heart's-cage-made-visible—

Ways of Entering Water

Headfirst or feet first. Coaxed
········or coaxing another

as if to woo a hesitant lover. *Come closer,*
········we say, *the water is fine.*

Graceless or tentative we move from
········one state of matter

to another that proves the body
········might be buoyant. *Hurry up*

we'd call to our mother as she waded in,
········slowly, as I now wade in, slowly,

soles of my feet remembering
········grooved lines of sandbars,

made by water snakes, my brother claimed,
········a cohort of serpents

coming out at night to rake
········their silent rock gardens. And still,

the body's unthinking lift to the toes
········with every wave, becoming

one's own rocking boat. As children,
········we begged—ten more minutes,

five more to somersault and kick
········and test who could hold

their breath longest, perhaps still recalling
     that first brush with water,

first home that makes our bright atmospheres
     other. In each ear, the whorl

of a shell left behind, cup and funnel
     for the hidden inner ear,

and there—three small sacks to portion
     our balance, hold us upright

(see how they stir as you lean closer?)—
     swimming through thin air.

Instructions for the Binoculars

> *Just like the stars are different where you are, the birds are.*
> —May Swenson to Elizabeth Bishop

I eavesdrop on your instructions
for the binoculars, assuming
she asked, somewhere deep in Brazil,
sending guava and papaya as she did
to Miss Moore, and you, perhaps, wooing back
with the latest technology, a new
pair of eyes through which she might call
down the birds. I have wholeheartedly
idealized you both, have imagined dinner parties,
dewy walks in the arbor, even this word *arbor*
where I would normally say *garden,* and yes,
the dictionary calls it *Obsolete. a grass plot;
lawn; orchard.* You were whole continents
away from each other, not linking arms
like schoolgirls. Still, I have believed
you were writing to me.

———

15. *What is the Principle of Priority?*
    *the rule that considers as valid only
    the oldest available name to a taxon*
16. *What is synonymy?*
    *the existence of different names
    applied to the same taxon…*
19. *Why do bird names change?*
    science… constantly evolving

———

How precise to point out the white dot on the nose-
bridge, exact numbers to see far or farther—
or not—*A "6x30" for instance gives you
that much less magnification and width.* I know little of birds,
and last night stood dumb while hundreds circled
the chimney of a church down the block, counter-
clockwise, and each orbit another one dropped
down that throat until the wheel broke and left me
unutterably empty. *Life, friends, is exhausting.
We must not say so.* Instead—
I am thinking of unusual alliances,
of you, and Elizabeth's distance. Or Kumin
being warned off the effusive Sexton,
quiet sister to put on Anne's jacket after
the garage, the plumes a terrible angel
welcoming home.

———

I've said nothing about the stars we failed
to see, shooting stars, the news said, which we imagined
beyond the Lafayette lights, the smog
from the Staley corn syrup factory flung
across the Wabash. All night the courthouse plays this
recording we call *birds of prey* to scare pigeons from nesting
and I think *aren't they smarter than that?* And I think
I too fear. This darkness *not quite,* this *no one else out*
which means only the homeless man waits at the bus stop,
a lone student carries his bike up the steps. I fear

I have given you the wrong impression. I love this town.
I keep leaving this town. My mother takes out a book
and says, *Chimney swifts, migrating.*
This is what the sky looks like here.

Notes on the Appositive

>*Example: I want to go back to that place, <u>that small fishing village in Mexico</u>*
>
>*Yours: I want to go to back that place,* _____

That small fishing village
is a basket of tomatoes.

Yours is Lake Michigan,
carburetor, tandem
bicycle.

That small fishing village
is south of the Yucatan.

Yours is fresh water,
weeds, a jar of furred
moths.

That small fishing village?
No one lives there.

The dune grass, plowed,
means the whole dune
dissolves.

Can't you see the deep
fibers of roots?

Someone says, *This
was once a beach.*
Someone says, *The natives,*

the natives, oh
bring me a camera.

Watershed

1. (LaGuardia Airport, 2009)

We approach over water, uncertain
        of ground, or only certain of ground
in that way we once learned abstract numbers.
        Trust and awe. Trust and expectation.
This, *where the airport sits,* as though
        I know something of place,
of where to place this landing like a dock
        for the sky, suddenness of
concrete that will only become more concrete,
        skyscrapers we learn to inhabit.
Would that the water were enough,
        that we might wash our faces directly
in the river, wide and salt-licked by the tide.

2. (Riverkeeper)

Finally, the ruling to dredge the Hudson.
    Decades in court because *who knew
better?* The river an open absolution
    for over one million pounds
of PCBs, one hundred tons of poisoned
    sediment, sick to the bedrock.

*1938—General Electric (GE) considered dropping the
use of polychlorinated biphenyls (PCBs) because a study
revealed health and safety problems, but they did not.*

*April 22, 1998—shareholder meeting, GE CEO Jack
Welch claimed: "PCBs do not pose adverse health risks."*

Driving inland—Peekskill, Spackenkill—
    we cross bridges that demarcate
each watershed. Square metal sign.
    Phone number in case of emergency.

*2002—After battling for two decades to avoid the
cleanup. . . GE said it would begin testing for PCB
hotspots. . .*

May, 2009—Phase 1 dredging begins.

3. (Bard Rock)

Peaceful to lean against
      the rock's broad face,
moss slippery across the surface
      as we pause
to contemplate swimming,
      fish moving
as one in thick schools
      that whip back and forth
their flickering jackets, shooting
      the summer's translucence
back again to an aqueous sky.
      We lean into each other, small
beside the glacial boulder,
      its picturesque position belying
a commercial convenience:
      1905, the women descending
for luncheons of mussels and lobster,
      crustaceans blushing on ice
chopped from lakes by the hands
      that will make this a town.

And we too fan our faces before the river,
      cheeks lit like the servants'
switchboard or flush with the beauty
      or just *hot,* so damn hot,
and wishing we might trace this water
      to one hidden thread, promise
of iron and cold from the recently frozen
      but somehow still moving

I want to say *source* and mean
      this is drinkable. And the ground
(if we climb high enough), not leeched?
      Pushed far enough inland?
Upland? Irresponsible want.
      Irresistible spring that cares
nothing for what we have done,
      what it does in return.

Exploring the Island

Arrow-nosed signs point us
towards a cemetery, plot

the size of a single, square room,
headstones like loose teeth

in tall grass. Husband dead at sea,
sons to the Civil War, markers

the size of postcards for a series
of infant dead. Only one woman

passed thirty, surviving on the island
well into her seventies. Now, not even

the park service tends the graves,
tills the orchard. The men who follow

the lobster to sea don't turn
this direction—*They go to the coldest*

reaches in winter, a man at the diner
tells us. Alone on her island

the woman's ghost stirs winter apples
over a hearth of the hardest stone.

Tuning A

> *Schumann was speaking today of a curious illusion, of which he has been conscious for several days past . . . .*
> —Rubert Becker

At the river, he pressed
linen handkerchiefs
against each ear; but then,
when he blocked out that sound,
he saw the trees mouthing
frantically to one another.
Or it was wind. Or
the trees were mouthing
just to him—a whole scream
of branches. He knew
it was real in the night
when the tuning A woke him.
He knew Schubert's voice, back
from the dead. Or his mother,
from the dead, or his unborn
children, their lips
unbuttoned, their thin arms
swelling around him.
Too beautiful. His own skin
rang shrill and metallic.
The water cold as the hollow
before any sound.

Suspension

    They place a steel bar in the birthing room
and forty-eight hours into labor finds J. hanging taut
        as if at the prolonged nadir
of a chin-up, moment between

        reaching bottom and starting the last half ascent
the strained muscles allow. Two nights without sleep,
        the contractions batter her back to pained
consciousness every ten minutes (more/less).

    Later, we'll look at this photo:
J.'s face with its boyish bangs swept to one side,
        eyes closed as if she's conducting
some intricate music by memory and reaching

        now the hardest part has lost all awareness
of outside world, turned wholly towards song that
        not that she's trying to remember
but borne along by to a place we can't follow—

    her wife pulls her back, says,
Look at me, Baby. Says, *Breathe.*

    On the third day, I consider prayer.
These women have been through too much, Lord,
        I pray, because I am scared
this time they might break, and I call to a God

       my deepest subconscious still grudgingly pictures,
if not with white beard, then some far, ghostly father.
           Too much, I say, because my prayers
are no longer requests but indictments, raw fear.

       At home, R. has washed the hand-me-down
clothes, handmade sweaters, hats, blankets
           sent from friends.
She has spread them across a rack in his room,

       the olive and aquamarine they have chosen,
the clothes like so many bright flags praying his arrival.
           They have held his name
under their tongues for months.

———

       God said *Become flesh* and I fear it.
The swell and throb, knife edge set to skin.
           I fear the split nipples
of nursing and the deflated ball of the belly.

       My friends, though, have wanted this
birth beyond reason, have felt their mothering
           deep within long before
the phrase *Great with child.* They have wanted

       the birth without drugs because *Lord,*
they would feel this.

———

    It will be another full day before the boy comes.
The women will gather around the bed, hold J.'s legs
        when the epidural leaves
one side numb. What they recall

    is her breath—*Like a low, orca moan*—
sound from the sea scientists have long believed
        has meaning of its own, shadow
of a language ringing the hull,

    the waves again breaking over.

The Bathers

Owls Head, Maine

Two women billow in the blue-green water,
sunlight and morning, a rock face

obscuring however they got here,
middle-aged debutantes of the waves—

First we saw just the one, floating
on her back before hinging at the hips

like a jewel box clicking shut,
kicking her feet down to right herself,

then the other—and neither are trim,
neither lovely as you'd have them,

coarse hair loosely tied, waists slack
over rippling thighs as they laugh

and bob, bob and laugh—this movement
so free I envy the one's careless tread,

the other's soft kick from the shallows.

Late Winter

And already, almost Easter. Lilies
droop full-blown in the blue vase,
spilling their copper pollen.

The cat stains her paws
in the powder, doesn't notice,
so intent on watching a squirrel circle
up the pine, so intent on the place
where it disappears off one limb and over
the fence. She stares
long after it's gone, ears forward

under the lilies' large globes,
which are so much whiter than the snow
that melted three weeks ago, I can't
not think of the hymn
we used to sing—*Whiter than snow, yes,
whiter than snow.* And my great-grandmother,
a stern Dutch woman, whose
soft spot was a garden, any flower. Holding
the creased Psalter Hymnal high up
before this small still life.

The Coefficient of Longing

We assign this longing the letter O.
        Not algebra's X, its questioning Y.

O teacup! O cobweb! O my love falling
        asleep before me. It's the moon

I crawl towards, pinhole light
        as I scale the dark building.

Even children know how, multiplied,
        it turns all to itself—

The train whistle multiplied by $O = O$,
        The dog at the fence times O.

And *times,* we say. *I love you times a hundred,*
        times a million. Divide yourself

by this longing and the streets will crack
        in their confusion.

Still, the trains keep barreling past.
        When there's nothing left to try

I feed it a slim line of praise—
        shake out the rugs of its house.

The Piano

> *I can hear the music better where I sit than at the keyboard.*
> —Donald Justice

Thought like a black, lacquer
box where I place

maple leaves, for instance,
red seeping towards green

on the young tree that tap
taps my window,

and the tri-folded pages
from the mailman's bag,

and the last sand I shake
from the dunes. Add this

one low plane overhead,
Flying the pattern,

a student explains, how
they take turns practicing,

mostly landings. Then leave
the box's lid up—

for the plane's wide orbit,
for the crack of leaves as a car

passes by, for the day to become
some music less voice

than collage. The way each
finger finds a different place

on the keyboard and
all at once, somehow

making counterpoint,
somehow, birdsong and

the neighbor's screen door
clapping shut. Sky separating

down through the leaves the way
a river might split

across low, pebbled places,
the fallen branches fanning it

into stream and stream and stream.

Notes

"*Knife-grinder: Principle of Flickering* (1913)" is dedicated to Benjamin Kolp. The epigraph is from Jeannot Simmen's *Malevich, Life and Work* (Konemann, 2000), and the italics in the second section quote liner notes from the Opus Kura release of Casals playing Bach's Cello Suites (2003). "Eppur si muove," in the poem's final section, was supposedly muttered by Galileo following his trial.

"The Dove House" is indebted to Tony Harrison's *Winslow Homer in England* (Hornby Editions, 2004).

In "Intermezzo" and "Tuning A," the epigraphs are from *The Letters of Robert Schumann*, selected and edited by Dr. Karl Storck, translated by Hannah Bryant (John Murray, 1907).

"To Fanny Mendelssohn" quotes a variety of late-Victorian texts peculiarly interested in small-handed women. See *A New Woman Reader: Fiction, Articles, and Drama of the 1890's*, Carolyn Nelson ed. (Broadview Press, 2000), for several instances.

"Wintering (January)" quotes a wonderful Wikipedia entry on skunks.

"Instructions for the Binoculars" quotes *Dear Elizabeth*, a collection of poems and letters from May Swenson to Elizabeth Bishop (Utah State University Press, 2000), for the poem's epigraph and the first italicized line in the poem's third section. The third section of the poem also includes a misreading of John Berryman's "Dream Song 14." The second section is taken entirely from the "FAQ" page for the Comitê Brasileiro de Registros Ornitológicos' website.

"Notes on the Appositive" is a misreading of an exercise in *The Poet's Companion* by Kim Addonizio and Dorianne Laux (Norton, 1997).

"Watershed" quotes *The Riverkeeper: NY's Clean Water Advocate* website in its second section.

"Suspension" is dedicated to Jax and Renee Gardner.

In "The Piano," the epigraph is from Donald Justice's "Little Elegy for Cello and Piano" in *A Donald Justice Reader* (Middlebury College Press, 1991).